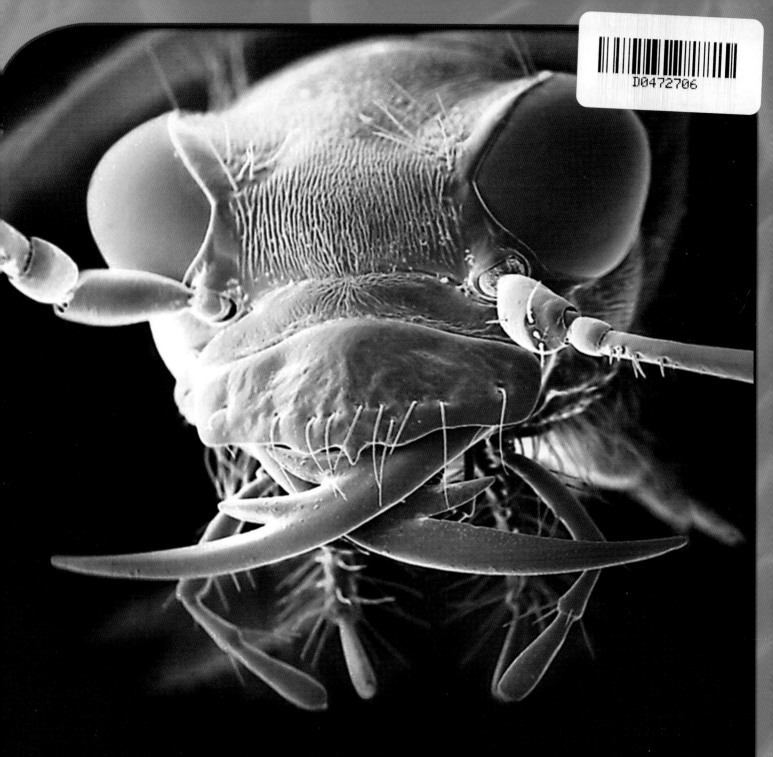

Extreme 3·D
Scary Bugs

Tiger beetle

Extreme 3·D
Scary Bugs

Bee head

Written by
Shar Levine and **Leslie Johnstone**

SEM and Light Microscope Photography by
Dr. Elaine Humphrey

Dedication

S.L. and L.J.—This book is for Ruth Lindsay.
She keeps our homes free from bugs and other
creepy-crawly things, and makes our lives so much easier.
We love you, Ruth.

E.H.—To Rex, Karen, John, and Murray
(entomologists at the Univerity of British Columbia)
and the Bug Lab Invertebrate Zoo for the wonderful
willing assistance and appreciation for insects they
pass on every day. They are always happily willing to
share mines of information.

Silver Dolphin Books

An imprint of the Advantage Publishers Group
5880 Oberlin Drive, San Diego, CA 92121-4794
www.silverdolphinbooks.com

Text copyright © 2005 by becker&mayer!
Extreme 3-D: Scary Bugs is produced by becker&mayer!,
Bellevue, Washington

www.beckermayer.com

If you have questions or comments about this product, send e-mail to infobm@beckermayer.com.

ISBN-13: 978-1-59223-365-6
ISBN-10: 1-59223-365-1

Produced, manufactured, and assembled in China.

2 3 4 5 09 08 07

06462

Edited by Don Roff
Written by Shar Levine and Leslie Johnstone
Designed by J. Max Steinmetz
SEM and light microscope photography by Dr. Elaine Humphrey
Illustrations by Roberto Campus, Ron Chironna, Dan Fell, Debbie Maizels, Erik Omtvedt, J. Max Steinmetz, and Christian Yah
Product development by Mark Byrnes
SEM colorization by Frank M. Young
Production management by Katie Stephens

Acknowledgments

Professor Murray Isman of the University of British Columbia, Pet Boutique, Jennifer Heron and the Bug Lab Invertebrate Zoo, Thoma, Charlotte, Sarah, Allen, Garnet, May, Jessica, Sumire, and John Swann. Thanks to Paul Rosenberg, and to Melissa Davidson and Alison Hunter for the way cool caterpillar. And to all our other friends who saved dead creatures found in their homes, stop bringing us bodies, please. We're done, at least for now.

Introduction

Do spiders have "combs" on their feet? Why do butterflies have "eyes" on their wings? The answers to these questions can be found in the fascinating pictures in this book. We used a very fancy electron microscope just so you could see up close and personal 3-D pictures of such things as spiders and butterflies. You will be able to marvel at a moth, go bug-eyed over a honeybee's eyes, and have a close encounter with a beetle. Best of all, these pictures will seem to jump off the page!

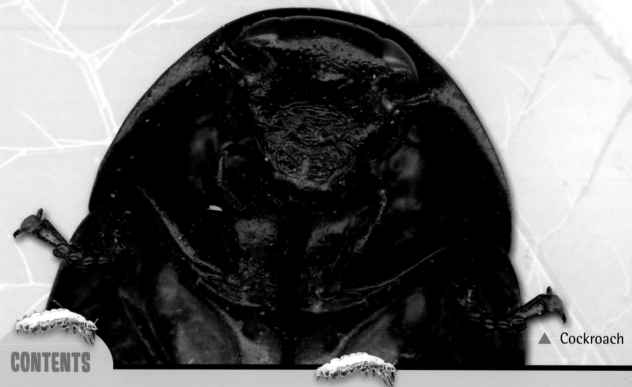

▲ Cockroach

CONTENTS

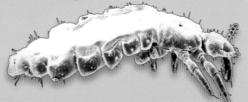

How We See in 3-D

We see in 3-D because we have two eyes. With both eyes placed at the front of our head, both eyes see the same object simultaneously and at slightly different angles. The position of our eyes also allows us to gauge distances easily.

For early humans, there were advantages to being able to judge distance. It makes it both easier to catch your dinner and avoid being made into lunch by wild beasts. Other animals—such as predatory birds that hunt for food—also have eyes at the front of their heads. Animals such as horses or cows, which graze and don't have to hunt for food, have eyes at the sides of their heads for a better view of potential predators. They simply need to see movement.

Some people can't see in 3-D. They may only be able to see with one eye, or they may not have the ability to combine the images seen with each of their eyes. These people must rely on other visual clues, such as position, size, or the way objects move, in order to judge distance. These are the same clues we use when we look at two-dimensional photographs, paintings, movies, or television.

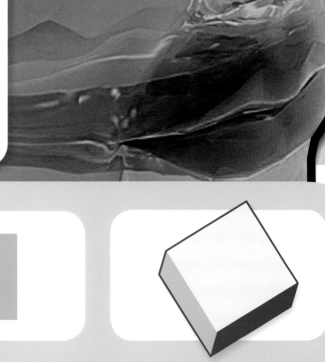

WHAT IS 3-D?

The "D" stands for "dimension," which is a measure in a single direction.

1-D: a line has one dimension, as it extends in a single direction.

2-D: a flat surface that has length and width, but no depth. In other words, two dimensions. An example of this is a painting or photograph.

3-D: an image that has length, width, and depth. Objects seen in 3-D look almost real.

The Red-Green Show

When you go to the movies, the images you see on the screen are flat. Some movies shown in special theaters (or with special projector lenses) feature 3-D effects, where things seem to fly off the screen and float in front of you. Some of these images are so real, viewers put their hands out and try to touch things that seem only inches away from their faces! To watch these 3-D movies, you have to wear special glasses. Some of these glasses have polarizing lenses that are dark gray, while other glasses have one red lens and one green (or blue) lens. These glasses allow the viewer to see the special effects.

Without the glasses, the image on the screen would be fuzzy—it would have a double image or appear to be outlined in red and green (or blue). Using the glasses allows each of your eyes to see a single, separate image. The pictures made using the red-green blurred outline are called *anaglyphic prints*.

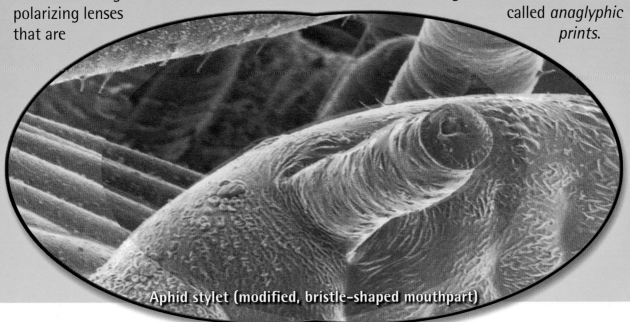

Aphid stylet (modified, bristle-shaped mouthpart)

The History of 3-D

It's hard to believe that the method you are going to use to view the exciting pictures in this book has been around for over 160 years! Sir Charles Wheatstone invented stereoscopic viewers in 1838. He got the name for his invention from the Greek words *stereos*, which means "solid," and *skopein*, which means "to view."

The invention of daguerreotypes, an early type of photograph, allowed Wheatstone to use stereo photographs in his viewer. These viewers and stereoscopic pictures were inexpensive and nearly every household owned one. They were used by both adults and children to view pictures from countries all over the world. As time went on, the pictures became geared toward kids—they depicted children's stories and fairy tales.

Stereoscopic viewer ▶

Microscopes

You may have used what is known as a compound light microscope. These microscopes are the type usually found in schools and homes. You look through an eyepiece to view a sample and see the light that shines from below the sample or onto the sample from the side. Compound light microscopes are very useful devices for seeing small objects. They are capable of magnifying objects several hundred times. A good-quality microscope of the type found in schools can usually magnify an object 400 times. A very high-quality light microscope can magnify an object at least 1,000 times.

The kind of microscope used to create the pictures in this book is called a *scanning electron microscope* (SEM). SEMs work by using a narrow beam of electrons. As this beam of electrons hits the sample, secondary electrons are given off from the surface of the sample. These are picked up by a secondary electron detector, which sends the image to a monitor. The narrow beam of electrons is scanned across the surface of the sample, hence the name. As the surface of the specimen is scanned, a computer is used to put the entire picture together on the monitor.

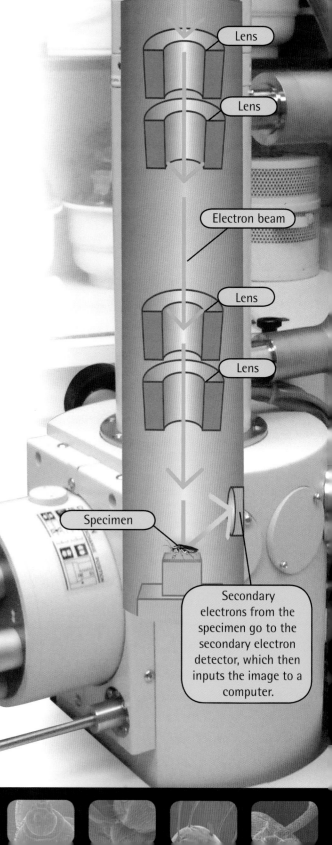

Electron gun (origin of beam)

Lens

Lens

Electron beam

Lens

Lens

Specimen

Secondary electrons from the specimen go to the secondary electron detector, which then inputs the image to a computer.

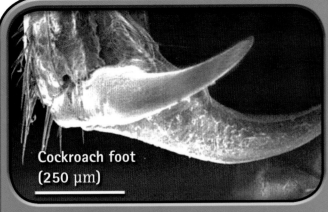

Cockroach foot
(250 µm)

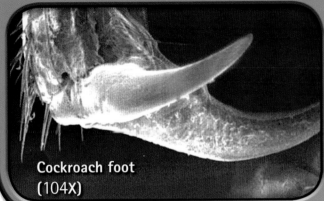

Cockroach foot
(104X)

WHAT'S THE SIZE?

When you see an image like the one to the left in an advanced science book, there is usually a scale bar and a number followed by the letters "µm" to indicate the size of the specimen in micrometers, or thousandths of a millimeter. This scale bar is a kind of ruler used to measure the specimen in the picture. Scientists can calculate how large the specimen is using this information.

Due to the complex math involved in converting the size of the specimen (in micrometers) to the size of the image in the book, we have instead indicated the number of times the image was magnified.

So, rather than the measurement being given as "250 µm," for example, it has been given as "104X" to show that it has been magnified 104 times.

In the lab

In the laboratory, scanning electron microscopes allow scientists to see the surface of objects in incredible, dramatic detail. Fine structures on the surface of plants and animals, individual cells, miniscule bacteria and viruses, and even some larger molecules all become visible. These microscopes have a wide range of uses, from product testing to nanotechnology.

Other uses include:

→ Forensics: comparing the surfaces of objects or identifying samples of materials too small to see.

→ Product testing: looking at materials to see if there are miniscule cracks.

→ Art: believe it or not, there are some artists using SEM images as part of their artwork.

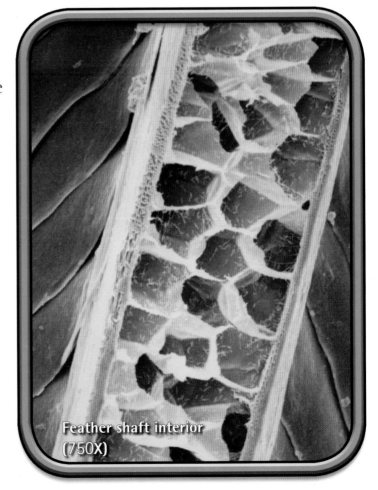

Feather shaft interior
(750X)

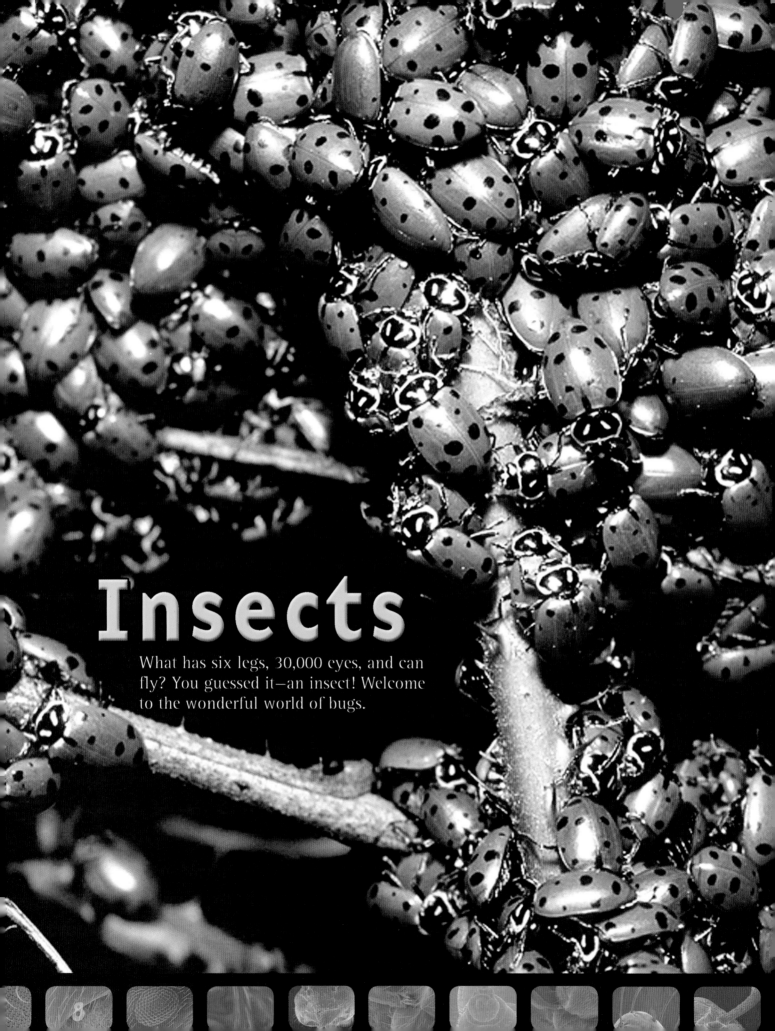

Insects

What has six legs, 30,000 eyes, and can fly? You guessed it—an insect! Welcome to the wonderful world of bugs.

ANATOMY OF AN INSECT

Insects have three main body parts: the head, thorax, and abdomen. They also have antennae, as well as mouths that are made up of several parts.

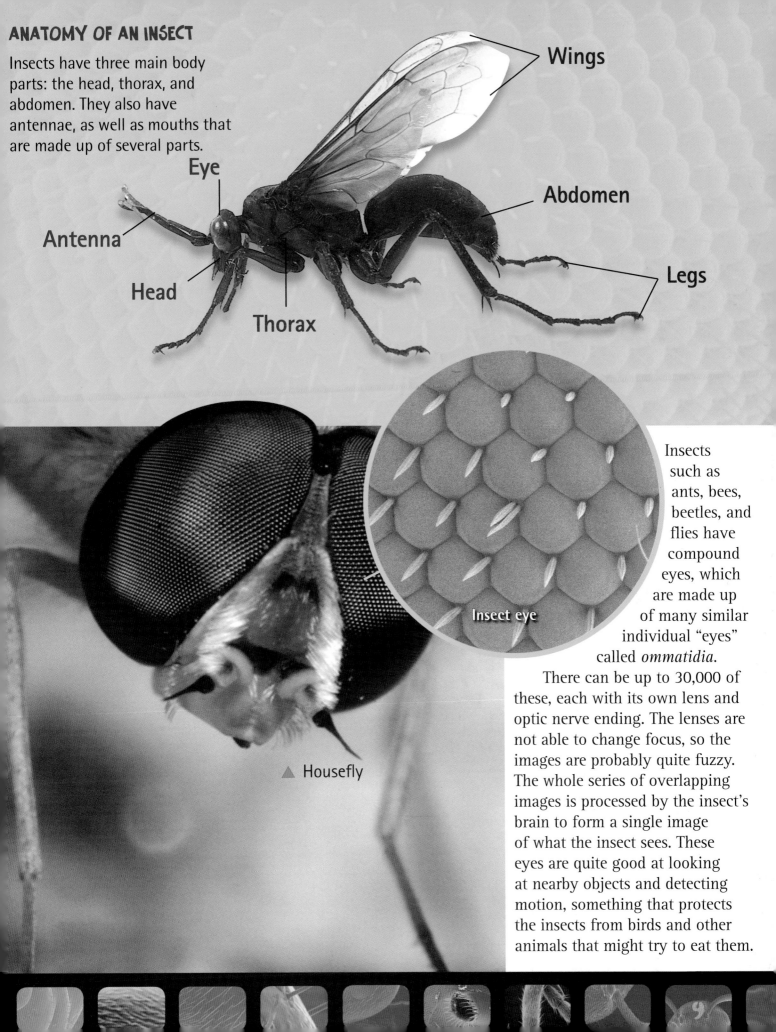

Wings

Eye

Abdomen

Antenna

Head

Thorax

Legs

▲ Housefly

Insect eye

Insects such as ants, bees, beetles, and flies have compound eyes, which are made up of many similar individual "eyes" called *ommatidia*. There can be up to 30,000 of these, each with its own lens and optic nerve ending. The lenses are not able to change focus, so the images are probably quite fuzzy. The whole series of overlapping images is processed by the insect's brain to form a single image of what the insect sees. These eyes are quite good at looking at nearby objects and detecting motion, something that protects the insects from birds and other animals that might try to eat them.

Ants

While spiders (page 44) and beetles (page 16) tend to live alone, ants live in colonies—some of which have up to 50,000 or even 500,000 of these tiny creatures. It is estimated that a large ant colony can eat more than 100,000 bugs or larvae in a single day.

Ant with egg bundle (58X)

If a colony is destroyed, the workers will risk their own lives to move the eggs and find them a new, safe haven. Compare the size of the egg bundle to the tiny size of this worker ant.

Ant colonies are like miniature cities: vast tunnels under the ground connect various parts of the colony. There are even ant highways that run between different ant nests! These ant cities may be 50 feet in diameter and 20 feet deep. Colonies have queens, soldiers, and workers. The workers vary in size according to their type and the job they do in the colony, such as gathering and storing food, raising the young, and taking care of the queen.

Soldier ants are usually larger than the worker ants and defend the colony from intruders with their strong jaws. They will swarm and attack anything that may wander too close to the nest. Ants can kill small birds and even snakes that have strayed too close. Certain kinds of ants—like the fire ant—have a chemical sting that can irritate your skin.

Ant (90X)

**Ant anus
(30X)**

Guess where this interesting structure is on the ant's body. Ants are so tiny that you would never see this part of the insect without the use of a powerful microscope. As with any living creature, food that goes in must be digested and come out somewhere. This is the ant's anus.

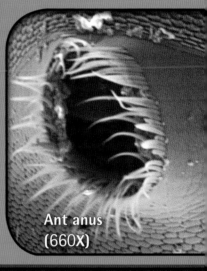

**Ant anus
(660X)**

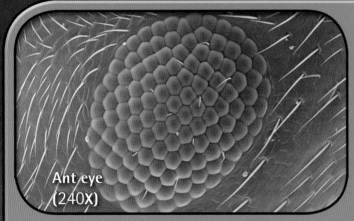

**Ant eye
(240X)**

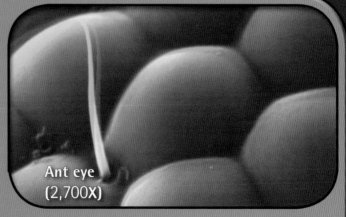

**Ant eye
(2,700X)**

Ants have compound eyes, which are small and have few facets. This is because ants don't need to see as well as many other insects. A few fine hairs stick out between the facets, and are used as additional sensory devices. Vision may not be as important to ants as it is to many other insects. Instead, ants have other ways to signal members of their colony. When ants meet members of their group, they groom each other with their antennae and exchange droplets of liquid containing *pheromones*. These liquids have various odors, which are used as chemical messages to communicate things such as the location of food.

Aphids

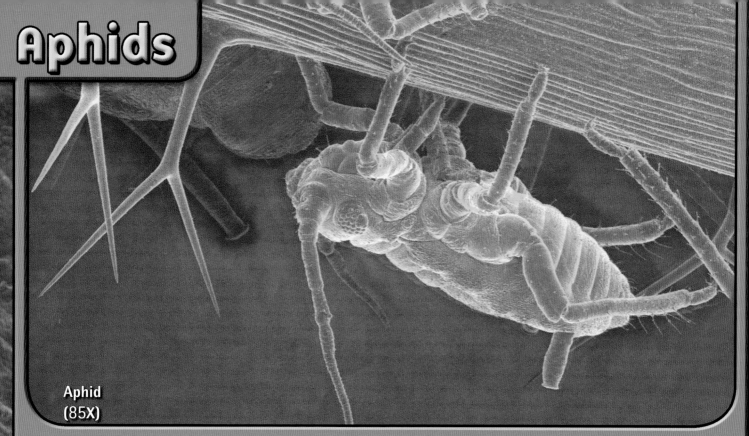

**Aphid
(85X)**

What is that tiny green bug crawling on the leaves of your houseplant? Probably an aphid! Using their piercing, sucking mouthparts to nourish themselves on plant sap, aphids are soft-bodied insects that usually live on the undersides of plant leaves. Because of excess sap removal by swarms of aphids, leaves can turn yellow or wilt. Aphids usually will not feed on healthy trees and shrubs.

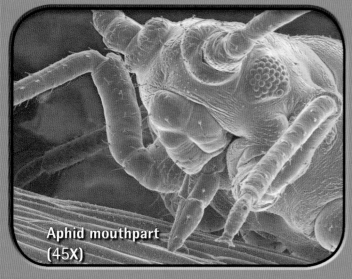

**Aphid mouthpart
(45X)**

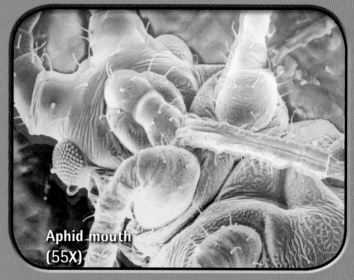

**Aphid mouth
(55X)**

Aphids belong to the order Hemiptera, which includes insects that have sucking mouthparts, such as cicadas and leafhoppers. Designed for sucking the sap from plants, the aphid's mouth has four long, sharp needles protected by a coating. These needles pierce through the outer surface of the stem or leaves and are used like straws. The aphids then drink up the nectar from inside the plant—like a vampire drinking blood from its victim's neck!

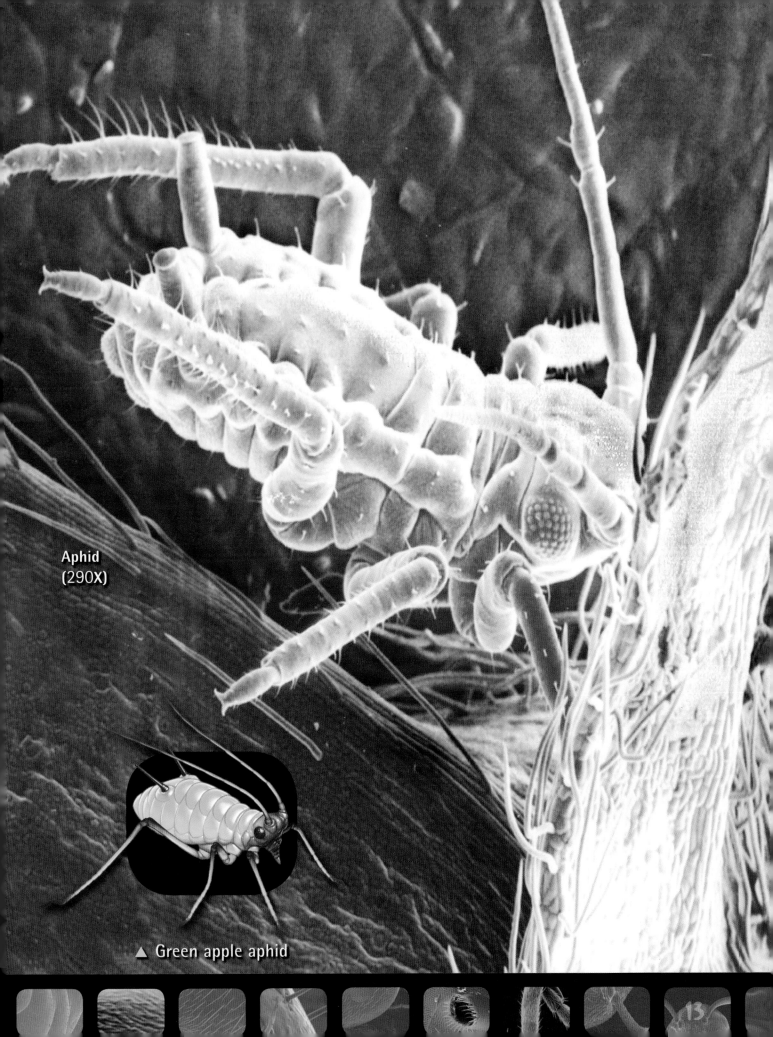

Aphid
(290X)

▲ Green apple aphid

Bees

Watch out! That fuzzy yellow-and-black blob in the middle of a flower just might be a bee. While you may think that bees are scary, they are also one of the most useful insects. Honeybees gather nectar from flowers. The bee's mouthparts are used like a spoon to scoop up the nectar. Bees carry nectar back to the hive in their stomachs. When they get to the hive, they spit it back up. Other bees working in the hive process the regurgitated nectar and seal it in beeswax containers. Only bees make honey.

▲ **Adult honeybee**

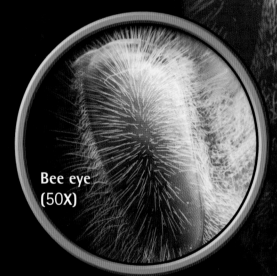

Bee eye (50X)

Bee head (1,350X)

Bees see in colors, especially yellow, and they also see ultraviolet light. In fact, some flowers have "bee guides," which are ultraviolet markings that direct the bees to the pollen and nectar in the flower. Honeybees are the only bees with hairy eyes. In bright sunlight, the hairs cut down on the glare.

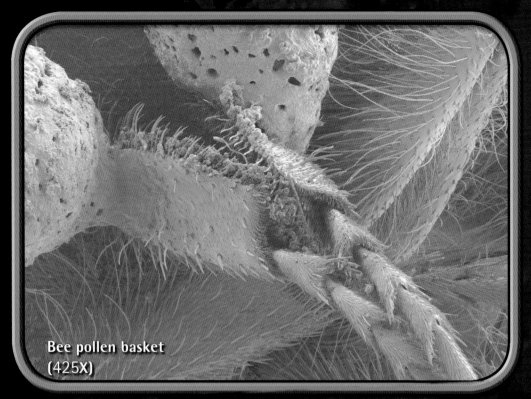

Bee pollen basket
(425X)

While bees collect the nectar from flowers, they also transfer pollen from one plant to another. The vibration from their buzzing loosens the pollen, which falls onto their fuzzy bodies. They collect the pollen from their body hairs and store them in pollen baskets.

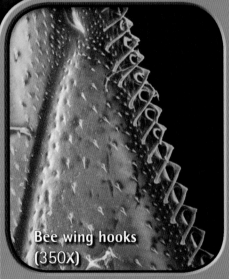

Bee wing hooks
(350X)

Bee wing hooks
(1,800X)

Bees have two pairs of wings that are hooked together in the middle so that they act like a single pair. They beat these larger attached wings about 200 times a second when flying. Bees can't fly if their body temperature goes too low.

Bees are cold-blooded, so when the temperature outside goes down, their blood gets colder. To keep warm, bees utilize a form of shivering that involves vibrating the muscles it uses for flying, but without any wing movement.

Did you know?

Honeybees are communal insects—they have a very highly developed social order. Some bees are workers, some are drones, and there is usually one queen in each hive. The queen bee can be identified easily, as she is bigger than the other bees. She is fed a special food called "royal jelly." Small glands in the mouth of the queen give off a chemical called "queen bee substance," which attracts the other bees to the queen if the bees swarm and move to a new location. Beekeepers now use this substance to attract bees to orchards or to trap swarming bees.

▲ Queen bee

Beetles

Beetle mouths are made up of several parts, which helps them chew their food. Tiger beetles are unusual because their large and well-formed mouthparts, which they use for chewing worms and snails, are directed downward. Watch out, though—this beetle uses its sharp mandibles for defense and it can bite you, too!

▲ **Adult tiger beetle**

Beetles, like ants (page 10), have compound eyes. Because beetles are slower-moving ground insects, like ants, they need fewer facets sticking out of their eyes. The facets on the eyes are used to detect motion and nearby objects, much like "curb feelers" work on an automobile so the car does not collide with the curb. Flying insects, such as bees (page 14), require more facets due to their rapid movement.

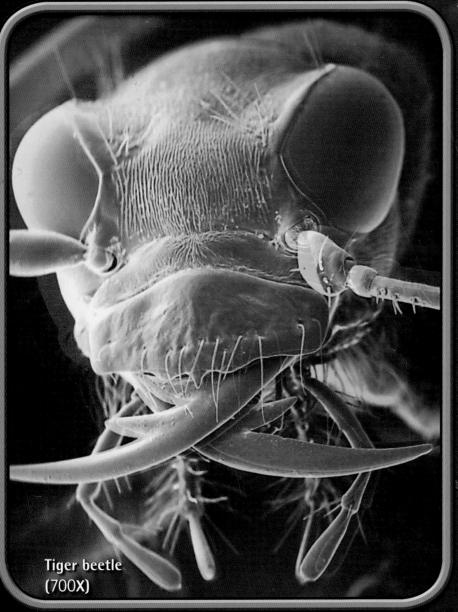

**Tiger beetle
(700X)**

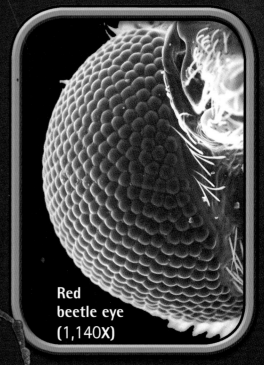

**Red
beetle eye
(1,140X)**

Red beetle molt ▶

Beetle foot
(70X)

Would you like to be able to smell with your feet? Beetles can! A beetle's shell is like a suit of armor, but the beetle still needs to know what is going on outside. One way that beetles do this is with sensory hairs—found mostly on a beetle's antennae. They are also on the beetle's legs or feet. Some hairs are used to feel the area around the beetle, while others detect chemicals or odors.

Red beetle
(70X)

Tiger beetle elytra
(700X)

Beetles and other insects don't have bones like humans. Beetles have a hard shell, or *exoskeleton*. This shell—combined with the shape of the beetle's body—makes it stiff enough to support the wings, yet light enough to allow the beetle to fly.

Despite the large size of some beetles, all these insects can fly. Adult beetles usually have two pairs of wings. The front pair forms a heavy cover or wing casing called the *elytra*, which protects the delicate back pair of wings.

Butterflies

Butterflies have a homing instinct. It's not quite like salmon swimming upriver to spawn, but butterflies will return to the same type of plant they were born on to lay their eggs.

Most people think that butterflies are the most beautiful insects. They float gently past you in the garden, shimmering with iridescent color in the sunlight. You can plant special kinds of flowers to attract butterflies to your garden. Butterflies particularly like nasturtiums, larkspur, pennyroyal mint, thistles, bergamot mint, and the appropriately named butterfly bush.

Butterfly wings are covered with millions of tiny overlapping scales that are often brightly colored and reflective. They sometimes have patterns that look like eyes. These "eyes" are used to frighten away birds that might try to eat them.

Butterflies have two pairs of wings: the forewings and the hind wings. The scales of the wings hold pigments, which reflect the light and give the butterfly its beautiful colorings. The colors have a purpose. Butterflies with yellow, orange, or red markings on darker backgrounds are trying to tell their predators that they aren't very tasty. Some butterflies take on these colors to fool predators into thinking that they won't provide a yummy meal, either. This is called *Batesian mimicry*.

▼ **Monarch butterfly**

△ **Monarch butterfly wing**

Butterfly wing scales (280X)

Proboscis (210X)

Proboscis (70X)

A butterfly doesn't have any teeth. Instead, it has a long, coiled proboscis. A proboscis is like a giant flexible straw that can be inserted into plants to drink nectar or even water. When the butterfly is not eating, it is coiled up tightly. When a butterfly finds food, it uncurls its proboscis—just like one of those coiled paper noisemakers you blow into at birthday parties.

Next to bees, butterflies can see the largest color spectrum— they can even detect ultraviolet light. Butterfly eyes are compound, with thousands of simple eyes to help the insect find food or identify danger.

Butterfly head

Caterpillars

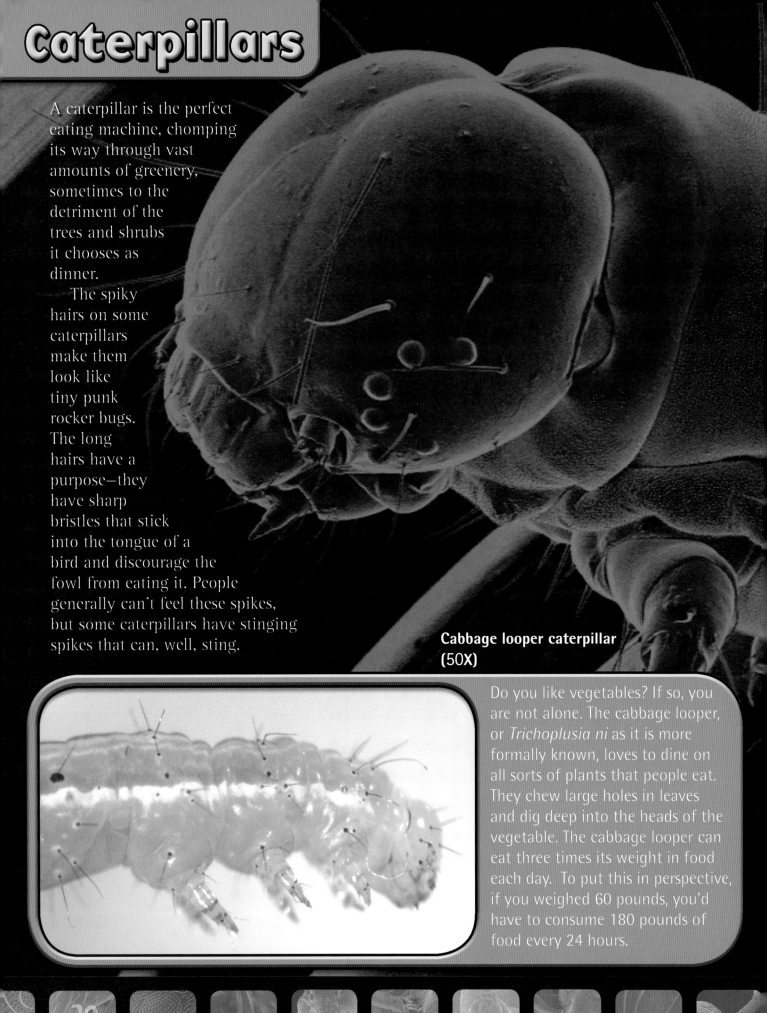

A caterpillar is the perfect eating machine, chomping its way through vast amounts of greenery, sometimes to the detriment of the trees and shrubs it chooses as dinner.

The spiky hairs on some caterpillars make them look like tiny punk rocker bugs. The long hairs have a purpose—they have sharp bristles that stick into the tongue of a bird and discourage the fowl from eating it. People generally can't feel these spikes, but some caterpillars have stinging spikes that can, well, sting.

Cabbage looper caterpillar (50X)

Do you like vegetables? If so, you are not alone. The cabbage looper, or *Trichoplusia ni* as it is more formally known, loves to dine on all sorts of plants that people eat. They chew large holes in leaves and dig deep into the heads of the vegetable. The cabbage looper can eat three times its weight in food each day. To put this in perspective, if you weighed 60 pounds, you'd have to consume 180 pounds of food every 24 hours.

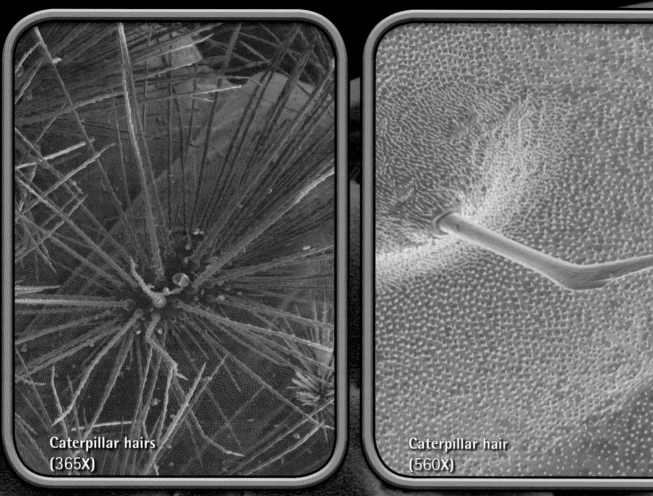

Caterpillar hairs
(365X)

Caterpillar hair
(560X)

Caterpillars come in many different shapes and sizes. Some caterpillars have soft hairs while others have stiff spines. These projections also vary—some are long while others are short. Some caterpillars have hair all over their bodies and others have a few tufts.

Did you know?

A stinging caterpillar has barbs or hooks on its bristles. These bristles are hollow and connect to a poison sac. If you touch one of these caterpillars, it releases its venom into its bristles and jabs them into your skin. This can hurt! There are over 10,000 kinds of caterpillars in the United States. If you don't know which kind of caterpillar you have encountered, don't pet it—just in case it's the stinging kind!

Centipedes

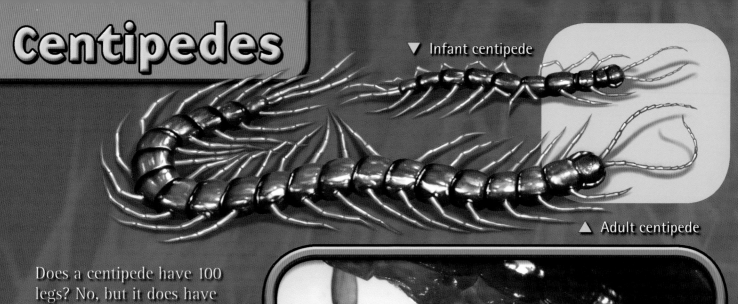

▼ Infant centipede

▲ Adult centipede

Does a centipede have 100 legs? No, but it does have more than six, which means it's not an insect, it's a *chilipod*. How many legs do they have? That depends on its age. When they are born, centipedes have only 14 legs, but full-sized adult centipedes have about 44 legs. However, they usually have only three legs on the ground at any one time when they walk.

▲ Centipede legs have four segments.

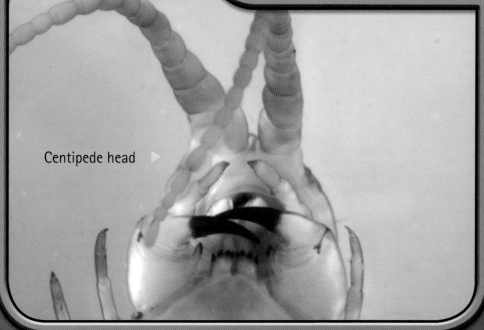

Centipede head ▶

Centipedes aren't fun things to keep around. They have a set of perforated claws that they use to clasp their prey before injecting it with poisonous venom. These claws are modified legs—and as we have noted, centipedes have lots of extra legs.

Compare this centipede to the millipede on page 37. Can you see any obvious differences? A centipede's body tends to be flatter, while a millipede is more rounded. The centipede has only one set of legs on each of its segments, while the millipede has two.

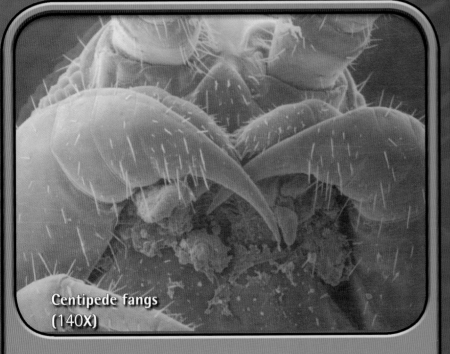

Centipede fangs (140X)

Unlike millipedes, which are vegetarians, centipedes are carnivores. They have claws and inject their prey with poisonous venom. Small birds, rodents, and even some reptiles can be dinner for a centipede. In a pinch, a centipede will eat dead animals as well. Centipedes are nocturnal, meaning they only like to come out at night.

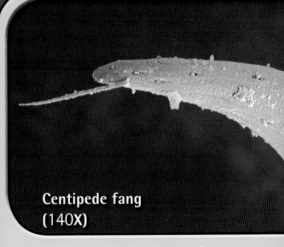

Centipede fang (140X)

Did you know?

Despite their scary appearance, centipedes are considered harmless to humans. Though most in the United States do not bite people, a few tropical species will bite, causing painful wounds. The jaws of young ones are usually not strong enough to cause more than a slight pinch when biting.

Cockroaches

These pictures are about as close as most people want to get to a cockroach. Many people consider cockroaches to be among the world's yuckiest creatures. However, as you will see, cockroaches are interesting little critters!

When they are born, baby cockroaches look similar to adults. Throughout their lives, these insects shed their skin and grow new armor as they mature. Their hard outer shell is actually their skeleton. If you ever see a white cockroach, you are probably looking at a cockroach that has just shed its skin. While most cockroaches are black or brown, some tropical species can be brightly colored.

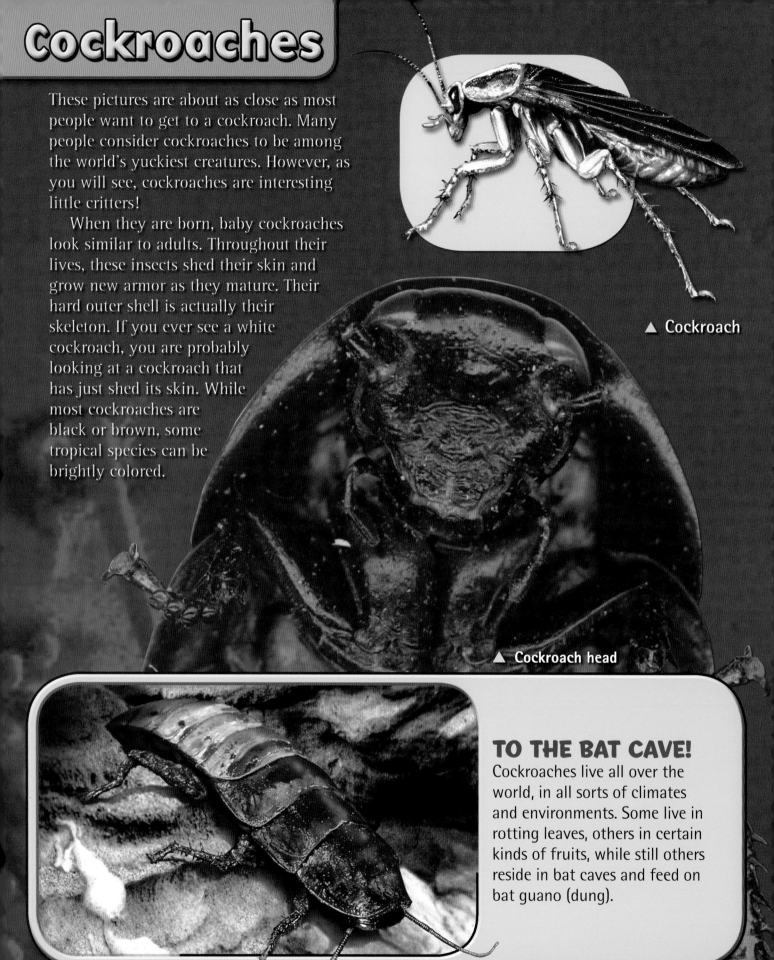

▲ Cockroach

▲ Cockroach head

TO THE BAT CAVE!
Cockroaches live all over the world, in all sorts of climates and environments. Some live in rotting leaves, others in certain kinds of fruits, while still others reside in bat caves and feed on bat guano (dung).

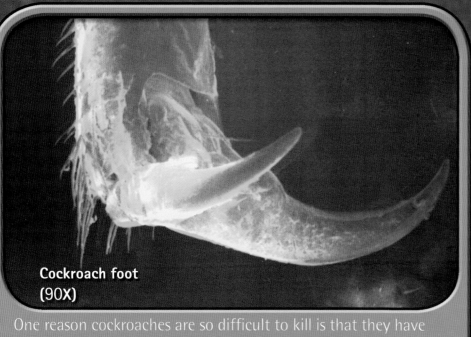

Cockroach foot (90X)

One reason cockroaches are so difficult to kill is that they have built-in motion detectors. Hairs on their feet and body dectect even the tinest vibrations that warn cockroaches if someone or something is trying to sneak up on them. When they sense danger, they can quickly dart away at speeds of up to three miles an hour. They can turn on a dime to change direction—as often as 25 times per second! They can also use the tiny claws on their feet to climb a wall and escape.

▼ **Rear cockroach leg**

▼ **Antennae**

The antennae of a cockroach also function as the insect's nose. The tiny hairs are sensitive to different chemical odors and help the cockroach find food and water. When cockroaches are trying to maneuver in the dark or in tight places, they use the tips of their antennae to brush along the surface and help them find their way.

Dragonflies and Damselflies

Dragonflies are among the most primitive insects in the bug world. If you listen closely, you can almost hear the other bugs saying, "Ha ha, you can't fold your wings on your body, but we can." But the joke's on the other bugs—the beautiful dragonfly can do amazing tricks. If you could watch a dragonfly in slow motion, you would see that the back wings move together and the front wings move up and down together. Using this unique system, the dragonfly can hover, fly forward, backward, and sideways, and maneuver much like a helicopter.

▼ Dragonfly

Dragonfly head (130X)

The dragonfly has enormous eyes. Just how big are these eyes? They are so large that they take up 90 percent of its head. These huge orbs allow the insect to see 360 degrees—in a complete circle. It's like being in a special movie theater with panoramic vision!

Dragonflies dine and dash! They have powerful claws on the ends of their feet so they can quickly snatch prey out of the air or on the ground. Just like when you go to a drive-through restaurant, dragonflies can grab a meal and go while in a hurry!

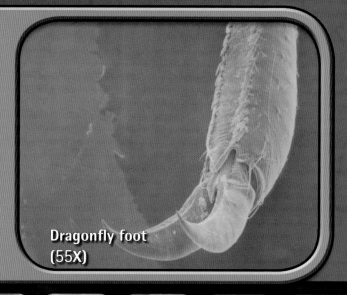

Dragonfly foot (55X)

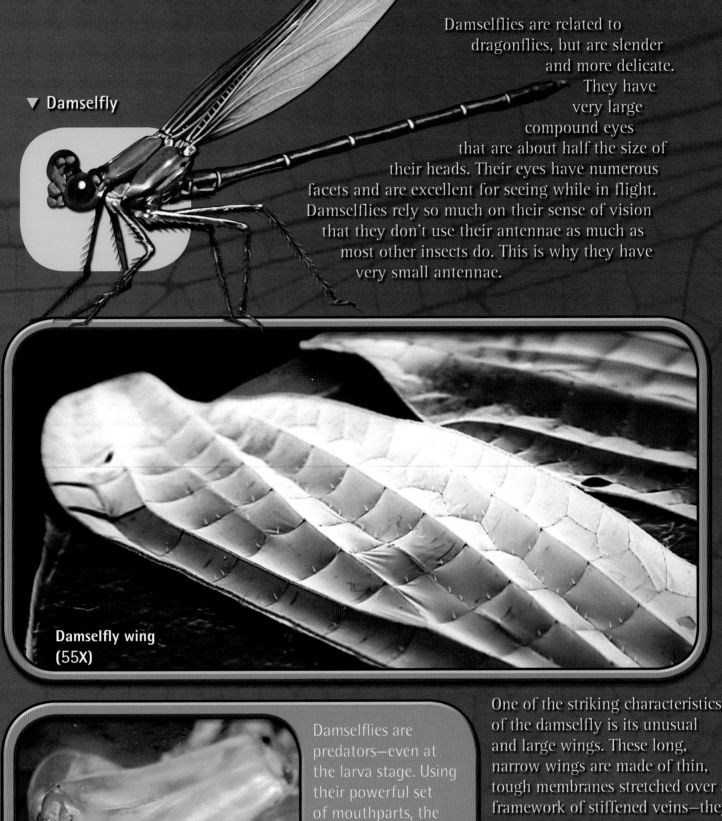

▼ **Damselfly**

Damselflies are related to dragonflies, but are slender and more delicate. They have very large compound eyes that are about half the size of their heads. Their eyes have numerous facets and are excellent for seeing while in flight. Damselflies rely so much on their sense of vision that they don't use their antennae as much as most other insects do. This is why they have very small antennae.

Damselfly wing (55X)

Damselfly larva head

Damselflies are predators—even at the larva stage. Using their powerful set of mouthparts, the immature damselfly can tear apart bugs caught near the water's surface and devour them easily.

One of the striking characteristics of the damselfly is its unusual and large wings. These long, narrow wings are made of thin, tough membranes stretched over a framework of stiffened veins—they resemble model airplane wings. When resting, damselflies fold their wings together over their backs. Because of their unique wings, damselflies and dragonflies are the best fliers in the insect world.

Earwigs

This is an earwig and you can understand why people might freak out when they see one. They look scary and their pincers look like the perfect tool for digging into small, dark spaces. They use their pincers primarily for defense against predators. Males have curved pincers, which are used mostly for carrying food; females have straight pincers, used mainly for defense.

Earwigs are omnivorous; they feed on live or dead insects, such as aphids, as well as living or dead plants. Though earwigs are not socially structured insects like ants and bees, the mother will both protect her eggs and take care of her babies for a few days. Earwigs are the only nonsocial insects to show this kind of maternal affection.

Earwig pincers (895X)

What are those scary-looking pincers? Will they hurt you? No. They are found at the earwig's back end and are used for defense. Take a closer look and you can see that they don't have ridges to clip or break objects that they are holding.

▲ Earwig

**Earwig head
(720X)**

Using their pincers, some earwigs can tunnel as deep as six feet to escape from the cold. Though harmless to humans, they are considered a pest, as they can damage gardens and infest homes. They are nocturnal, coming out mainly at night, but earwigs are also attracted to light.

"Did you hear about the kid who went camping, left his tent flap open, and an earwig crawled up inside his ear and laid eggs in his brain? No, really, it happened to my cousin's friend last summer!"
  This is just an old myth. Earwigs are harmless— they can't bore into your brain!

Flies

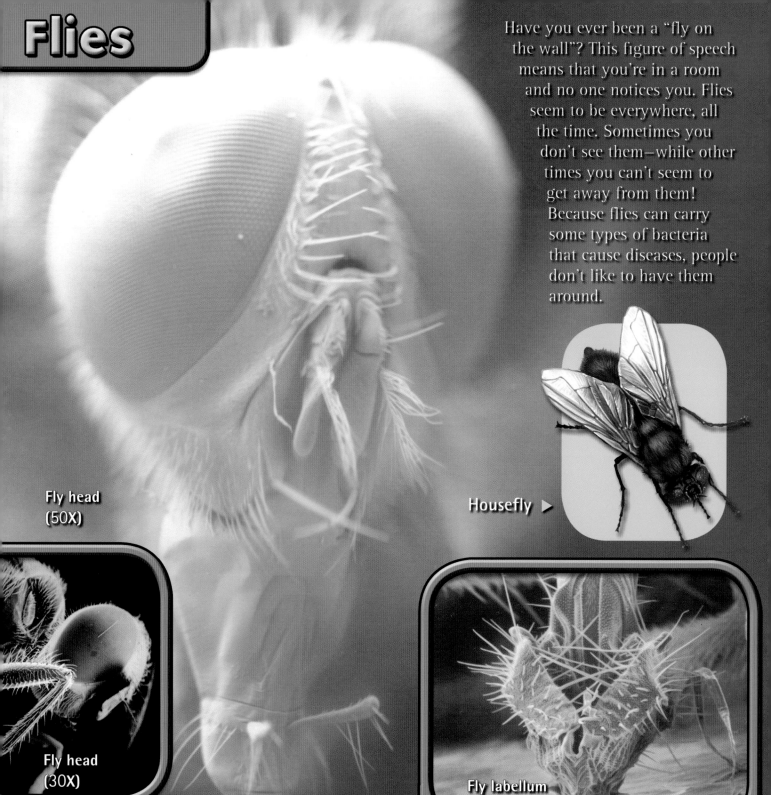

Have you ever been a "fly on the wall"? This figure of speech means that you're in a room and no one notices you. Flies seem to be everywhere, all the time. Sometimes you don't see them—while other times you can't seem to get away from them! Because flies can carry some types of bacteria that cause diseases, people don't like to have them around.

Housefly ▶

Fly head (50X)

Fly head (30X)

Flies vary in size from the tiny fruit fly circling overripe bananas to the huge horsefly that infests lakes and streams during the summer.

Fly labellum (105X)

A fly can tell if food is salty or sweet and will sponge up liquid food using its *labellum*, which is the hairy pad at the bottom of its head. When it finds a food it likes, it can leave behind a chemical so that other flies will be attracted to the food.

As you can see, flies have large eyes. These eyes give the fly a huge field of vision. If you've ever tried to swat a fly, you know that they are able to see your swatter coming from almost any direction—this makes them difficult to swat!

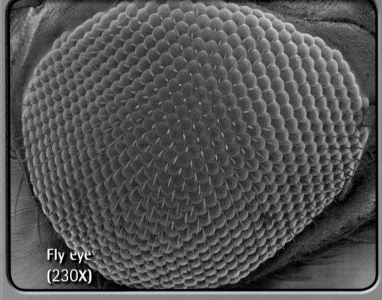

Fly eye (230X)

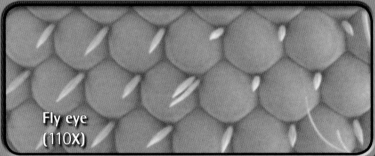

Fly eye (110X)

Fly foot (180X)

What would a fly be called if it couldn't fly? Would it be called a "walk"? Despite its name, a fly can also walk. Insects walk very well, as they have three pairs of legs. A fly's legs and antennae have hairs, some of which are touch receptors. If these hairs are touched or moved by air currents, the insect can sense it.

Fly larva anus (55X)

Maggot (fly larva)

There are over 16,000 species of flies. The common housefly begins life as a maggot, growing on rotting fruits and vegetables or dead animals. From larva to adult, the housefly lives for about 17 days.

June Bugs

This giant bug resembles the ancient scarab beetle found in Egypt and often featured in horror movies. The June bug, also called the May beetle (make up your mind—is it May or June?), spends most of its life underground as a crescent-shaped grub, feeding on grass. In May— no, make that June—the beetle comes out looking much like the one you see here.

▲ Male June bug

▲ Female June bug head

The helmetlike antennae of a female June bug resemble a samurai warrior's headdress.

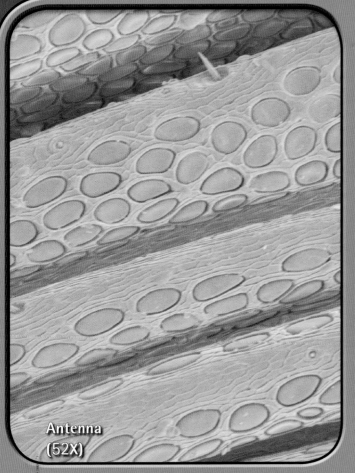

Antenna
(52X)

Antenna
(22X)

The June bug shown here is a *Polyphylla decemlineata*, or a ten-lined June beetle. These bugs usually have white or grayish lines along their bodies. Guess how many lines they have? If you answered "ten," you've been paying attention!

Leg
(30X)

If you're looking for a June bug, check out streetlights and bright lights around your house. These bugs don't move fast, so it's easy to catch one and study it. Though they don't bite, be gentle when handling them.

Newly hatched June bug larvae—also known as grubs—can often be found at night crawling on their backs. Approximately 8 to 40 millimeters in length, grubs must wait nine months until they molt and transform into adults. Grubs are primarily underground dwellers and can harm plants by eating the roots.

Ladybugs

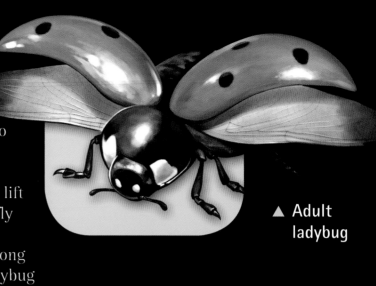

▲ Adult ladybug

These beautiful red bugs with black dots are a favorite with children everywhere. They look like friendly bugs, so nobody wants to squish ladybugs. However, these bugs are just a pretty variety of beetle (page 16). If you have a ladybug on your hand, blow on it gently. It will lift up its hard wing casings, unfurl its wings, and fly away home.

Tiny insects such as aphids (page 12) are among a ladybug's favorite meals, which makes the ladybug helpful to plant owners and farmers alike.

Because ladybugs are beetles, they have hard exoskeletons. At the start of their life cycle, a ladybug egg hatches and the baby that comes out is a soft, thick larva. If the larva was born with an exoskeleton, it would probably have to molt daily, since it grows so fast. Eventually, after lots of eating, the larva changes into a pupa and finally into an adult ladybug.

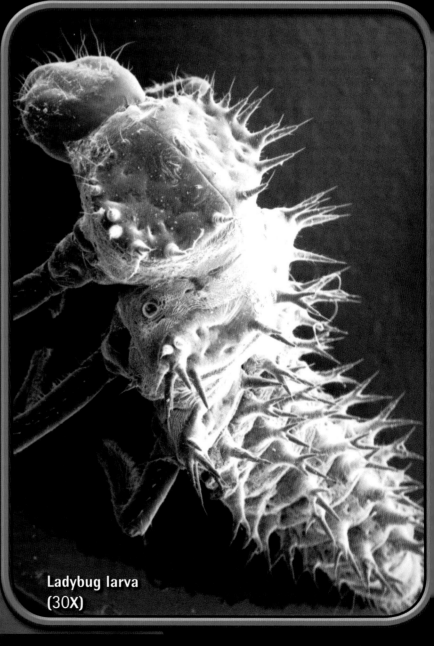

Ladybug larva
(30X)

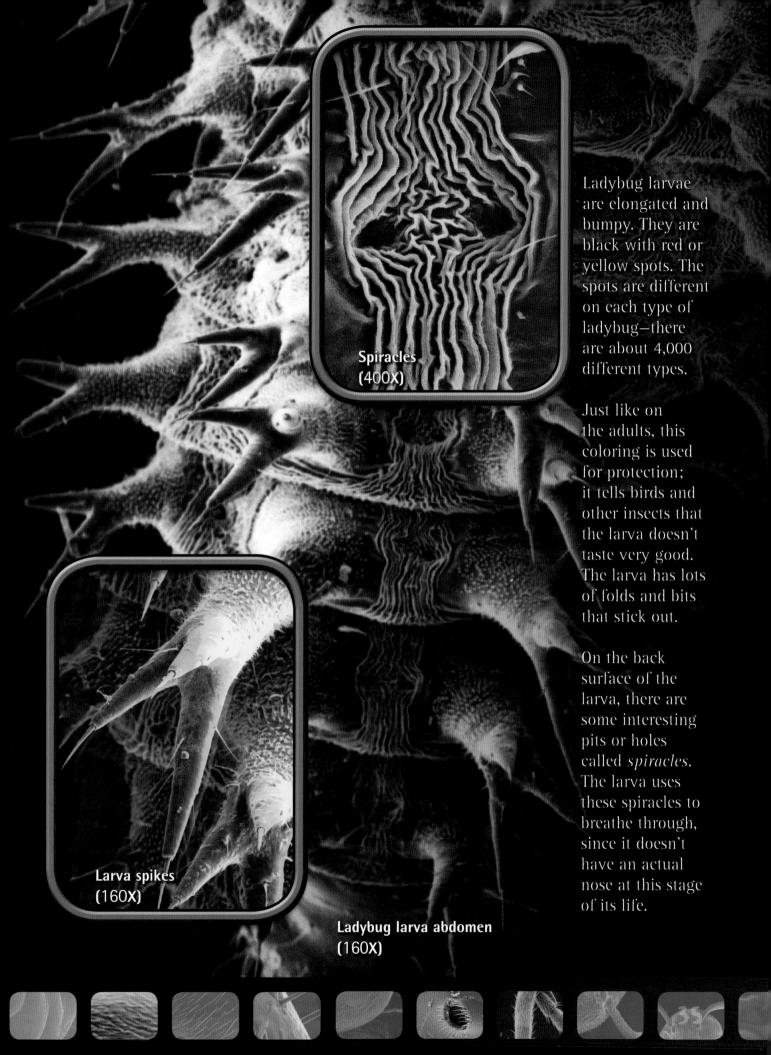

Spiracles
(400X)

Larva spikes
(160X)

Ladybug larva abdomen
(160X)

Ladybug larvae are elongated and bumpy. They are black with red or yellow spots. The spots are different on each type of ladybug—there are about 4,000 different types.

Just like on the adults, this coloring is used for protection; it tells birds and other insects that the larva doesn't taste very good. The larva has lots of folds and bits that stick out.

On the back surface of the larva, there are some interesting pits or holes called *spiracles*. The larva uses these spiracles to breathe through, since it doesn't have an actual nose at this stage of its life.

Millipedes

Do you look like any of your cousins? You may not live in the same city—or even the same state or country—but chances are you have some things in common with your relatives. Consider the millipede. Although it may be found crawling in your garden, it is related to lobsters and shrimp. Though you wouldn't want to sauté a millipede in garlic and butter for dinner, it is in the same family as these tasty crustaceans.

Leg segment (125X)

As a millipede gets older, it begins to molt, or shed its skin. Each time it does this, it gets more segments and more legs. Some of these creatures can live several years.

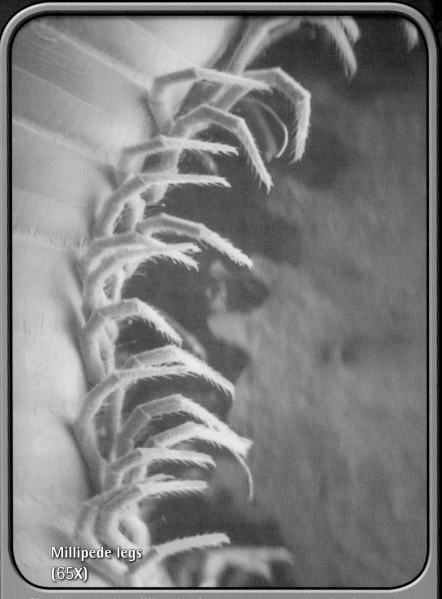

Millipede legs (65X)

Check out this millipede. As you can see, despite its name, it does not have a thousand legs. What it does have is two pairs of legs on each of its many segments.

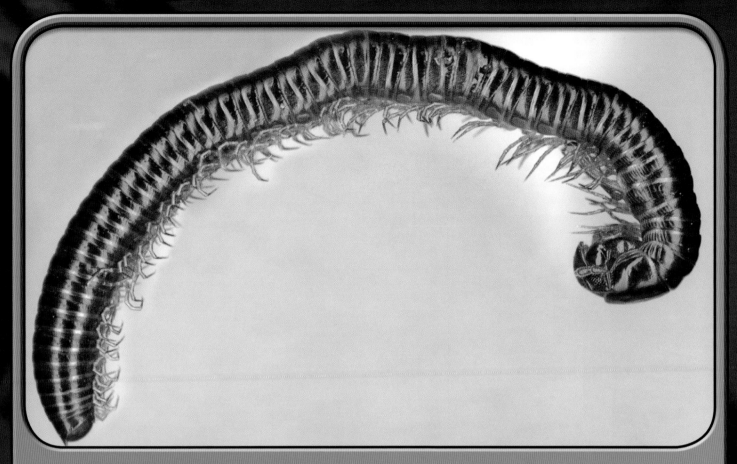

You can tell the age of a millipede by counting its segments. Do not pick it up to do this (see below). Young millipedes have less than seven segments and may have only a few pairs of legs.

Did you know?

Like most centipedes (page 22), millipedes are not dangerous to humans. While the millipede will not hurt you, it still isn't a great idea to pick one up and play with it.

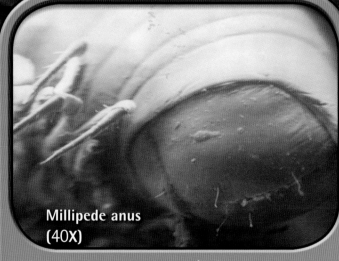

Millipede anus (40X)

Millipedes are detritivores (animals that eat dead organic matter, such as rotten fruit and leaves). After the food is processed, the waste material comes out of the millipede's anus. Some millipedes have glands that secrete, or give off, a liquid that can irritate your skin.

Mosquitoes

You're in bed, the lights are off, and you hear the familiar high-pitched sound of a mosquito looking for a warm body. BZZZZZZZZ. Ouch! You've been bitten. Sound familiar? Mosquitoes are a pain in the neck. They are also a pain just about anywhere they suck the blood out of you. Let's take a look at this pest.

Only a female mosquito can bite you—and technically, she doesn't have teeth, so it's not a bite. The mosquito has a chemical in her saliva that acts like a local anesthetic, taking the sting away from the area she is dining on. Because your blood is too thick to be sucked through her strawlike mouth, she releases a *vasodilator*, or a chemical that widens your blood vessels. A protein in her saliva is the reason for the swelling reaction on your skin.

Adult mosquito

This is a close-up of a mosquito's face. You can see the long mouthparts that she uses to pierce your skin and draw blood. Just looking at this makes you itch!

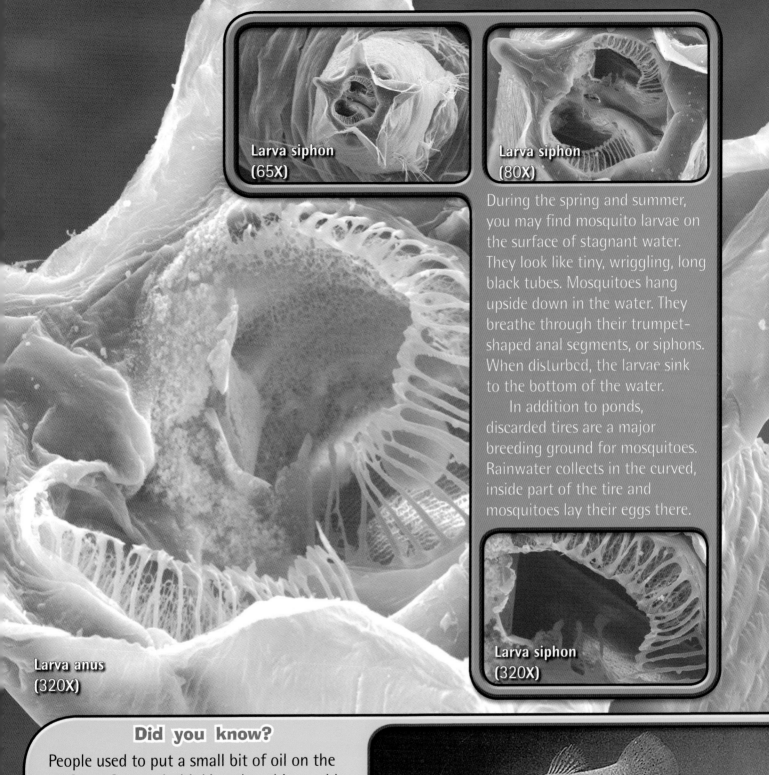

Larva siphon
(65X)

Larva siphon
(80X)

During the spring and summer, you may find mosquito larvae on the surface of stagnant water. They look like tiny, wriggling, long black tubes. Mosquitoes hang upside down in the water. They breathe through their trumpet-shaped anal segments, or siphons. When disturbed, the larvae sink to the bottom of the water.

In addition to ponds, discarded tires are a major breeding ground for mosquitoes. Rainwater collects in the curved, inside part of the tire and mosquitoes lay their eggs there.

Larva siphon
(320X)

Larva anus
(320X)

Did you know?

People used to put a small bit of oil on the surface of a pond, thinking that this would cut down on the mosquitoes because the insects couldn't breathe through this layer of oil. This was not great for the environment and could potentially harm fish, birds, and other bugs, such as dragonflies. Instead, people are now putting tiny fish called gambusia into the water. These type of fish love devouring mosquitoes.

Gambusia

Moths

There are several ways that you can tell butterflies and moths apart. Butterfly wings fold upward and moth wings fold backward. Butterflies generally fly during the day, while moths fly at night. Butterfly antennae are usually knobbed, while moth antennae are usually feathery or threadlike.

Moths have good memories. Adult moths will lay their eggs only on certain plants; these plants contain chemicals that the moths remember from their days as caterpillars. If a caterpillar tastes a certain plant chemical, the grown moth will return to a plant that contains the same chemical to lay its eggs.

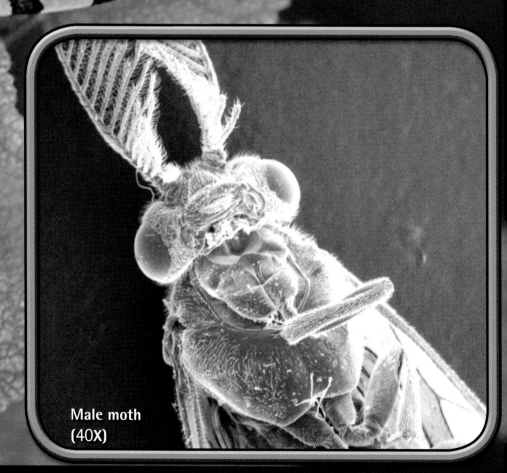

Male moth (40X)

Moth head
(90X)

As you've probably seen on your porch at night, moths are attracted to light, which they use to navigate. Moths navigate in two different ways: they use the moon and stars (if there are no porch lights) when available, and geomagnetic clues (the Earth's gravity field) when light sources are obscured.

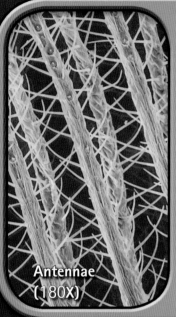

Antennae
(180X)

The feathery antennae you see here are found only on male moths. These large, fuzzy antennae can catch the scent of a female moth over long distances and—like the decorative feathers of a peacock—also help to attract a mate. Female moths have smaller, more threadlike antennae.

Moth scales
(60X)

SOLAR POWER

The current belief by scientists is that moth scales work as tiny solar heat collectors. Before flight, most moths must first warm up to about 80 degrees by absorbing the sun's heat directly onto their cold bodies.

Did you know?

The pupae of the yucca moth can survive for over 30 years and still be viable, which means that they are still capable of hatching. The pupa hatches only when there is enough water; if it is too dry, it stays in the pupa stage. When the rains come and there is sufficient moisture, the yucca moth hatches.

Praying Mantises

Some classic science-fiction movies feature massive killer insects that resemble mantises. However, in real life, these creatures are quite tame and don't sting or bite people (though their front legs can pinch). Mantises are beneficial insects in the garden, as they feed on plant-damaging pests like grasshoppers.

You know what a human skeleton looks like, especially if you go trick-or-treating. But have you ever seen a praying mantis skeleton? This is a molt of the insect. As the mantis grows, it sheds its outer layer and grows a new one.

Mantis molt

It doesn't take much imagination to see where the name "praying mantis" comes from. This creature is not religious; it only appears like it is at prayer. Mantises have forelegs that are razor-sharp and can firmly grasp prey in their grip. The mantis doesn't play with its food—it's pretty ruthless, biting into the neck of its prey and rendering it helpless. The word *mantid* is Greek for "prophet."

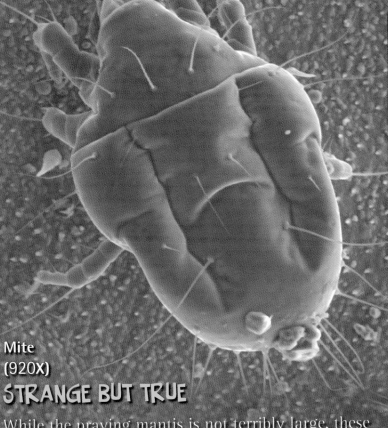

**Mite
(920X)**

STRANGE BUT TRUE

While the praying mantis is not terribly large, these little bugs are even smaller. When a family of mites wants to dine out, sometimes the mites choose the molt of a praying mantis for their main dish. Of course, the mantis isn't using the molt anymore, so it works out well for everyone.

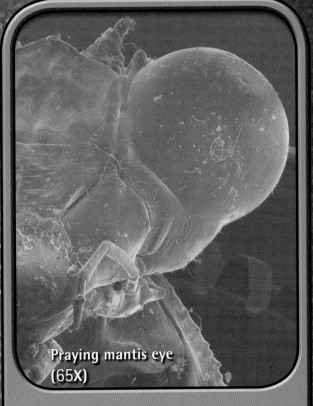

**Praying mantis eye
(65X)**

My, what big eyes you have! Turn your head and see how far your head rotates. If you were a praying mantis, you would be able to turn your head almost all the way around your body.

Spiders

Most people wouldn't like to get too close to a spider, but here's a great chance to study spiders from a safe distance. Contrary to popular belief, only a few spiders are very poisonous. This category includes the black widow, the brown recluse, and that large, hairy thing crawling on your shoulder now . . . just kidding!

Spiders are not insects; they belong to a group of animals called *arachnids*. Most spiders have eight eyes, although some are six-, four-, or two-eyed. There is even a one-eyed spider.

The jumping spider has the best eyesight. In fact, its eyesight is so good that it doesn't even spin a web to catch its dinner. The two large eyes in front help the spider to see its prey and the two small ones help judge distance. There are also two sets on each side of the head to help the spider see peripherally, or to the sides. The jumping spider can leap over 20 times its own length! If you were four feet tall and had this ability, you could jump over an eight-story building!

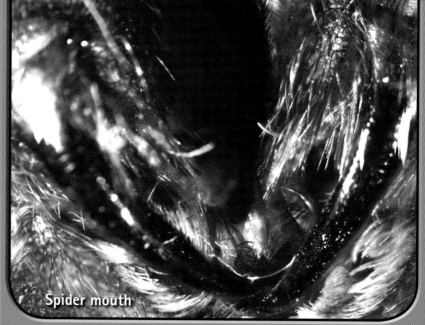

Spider mouth

Because the web is sticky, the spider's prey cannot get free. The spider then kills its victim with poison from its fangs and wraps it up in silk for dinner. Using a magnifying glass, you can see fangs on even a common garden spider. Your parents probably tell you to take small bites and chew your food before swallowing. Spiders don't chew their food at all. They suck out the liquid from their prey or dissolve their prey with enzymes—which come out of their mouths—and then suck out the dissolved prey. Spiders are very useful creatures because they eat a lot of insects. Without them, the world would be overrun with insects!

Jumping spider

Jumping spider

Each spider species has its own web pattern, designed to catch the kind of food that the spider likes to eat. Some spiders have webs that look like tunnels, while others have tube-shaped webs. Look around your house and garden and see if you can spot the different kinds of webs. House spiders make webs that are formed in sheets; garden spiders make webs that are shaped like orbs. Spiders don't have to learn how to make these webs—they are born with this knowledge. Contrary to popular belief, not all spiders spin webs.

Spider silk (360X)

Spinnerets (1,200X)

The spinnerets are the finger-shaped organs on the rear of a spider's abdomen that secrete the web material. The sticky spider web material comes out as a liquid protein, which hardens when stretched out in the air. Spiders can even produce different types of silk webbing for a variety of purposes.

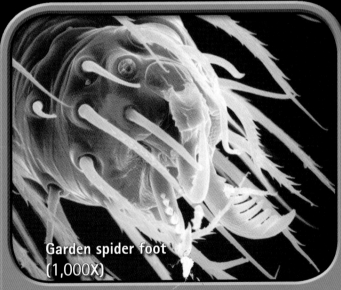

Garden spider foot (1,000X)

When the spider's prey touches part of the web, the spider feels the vibrations on the strand. Spiders, however, don't stick to their own webs because they secrete an oil that allows them to move freely along the web. The spider's feet and legs have small, comblike projections that are used to handle the web material when they are eating or when constructing new webs.

Did you know?

Found in South America, the Goliath birdeater can be up to one foot long and can trap and eat small birds and adult mice!

Wasps

When children are bitten by an insect, they will often say that they've been stung by a bee. Sometimes that "bee" is really a wasp. There are several ways to tell bees and wasps apart. Bees eat only nectar and pollen; wasps eat other types of food, such as the eggs or bodies of other insects or spiders.

▲ Adult wasp "yellow jacket"

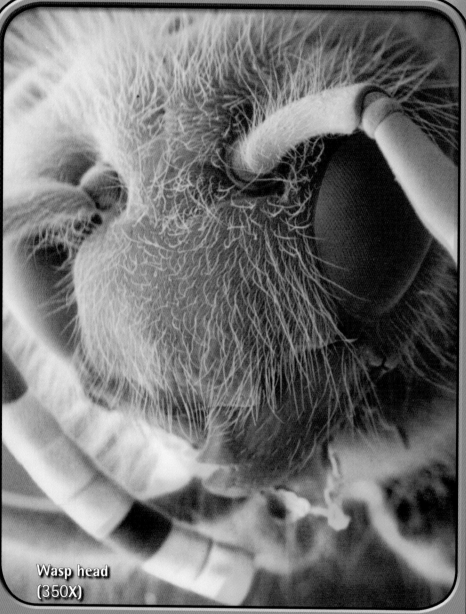

Wasp head (350X)

Wasps paralyze their live food before bringing it home to feed to their larvae. This is so their prey doesn't spoil on the way home. While both bees and wasps will construct homes for themselves, a beehive has chambers of beeswax for storing honey. Wasp nests can be made from chewed-up wood and look papery, or they can be made from mud.

Parasitic wasp (7X)

This picture of a parasitic wasp is an excellent example of 3-D. When seen with the naked eye, the picture is flat. When you look at the picture again—this time using the glasses—the wings jump off the page and you see the insect as if it were in front of you! This particular wasp also has very interesting markings on its wings, which look like eyes. This is a protective coloring.

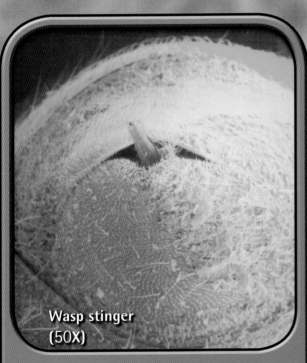

Wasp larvae (900X)

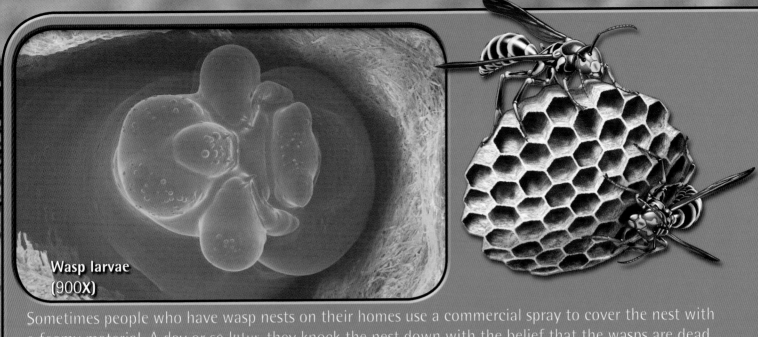

Sometimes people who have wasp nests on their homes use a commercial spray to cover the nest with a foamy material. A day or so later, they knock the nest down with the belief that the wasps are dead. Beware—the inhabitants of the nest may not be dead! Shown here is a small wasp nest that someone sprayed and knocked down. When it was placed under the hot lights of a light microscope, the heat caused the larvae to start hatching, much to everyone's dismay—especially the researchers operating the microscope!

Wasp stinger (50X)

Unlike a bee, which dies after stinging you, a wasp can sting a person repeatedly. A bee's stinger remains in your skin, but a wasp's stinger stays intact.

Wasp stinger (1,500X)

Glossary

Antennae: Twin projectiles on the head of an insect, used for smell and to sense motion.

Anus: The opening of an animal where food wastes are expelled.

Arachnid: A class of arthropods that includes scorpions, spiders, mites, and ticks.

Arthropod: A group of animals with segmented bodies, exoskeletons, and jointed legs.

Batesian mimicry: An act of mimicry, or imitation, of another species by an animal in order to avoid predators. Named after the English naturalist Henry Walter Bates.

Bristle: The spiny hairs on an insect or animal such as a caterpillar.

Colony: A nest or hive made by social insects such as termites, bees, and ants.

Elytron: The tough, horny forewing of a beetle or an earwig (plural: elytra).

Exoskeleton: The collective plates of a body that make up a hard outer shell.

Facet: The outer surface of each ommatidium.

Gambusia: Various small fish of the genus Gambusia that feed upon mosquito larvae.

Honeydew: The sweet liquid deposited on shrubs and trees, usually from the bodily wastes of aphids. Ants and other insects then consume it as food.

Hymenopterans: Insects such as honeybees and ants that have developed social systems where members of the colony are either workers, drones, or a queen.

Insect: A class of animal having three body regions—head, thorax, and abdomen—and in which the thorax has three segments, with each segment bearing a pair of legs.

Labellum: The lower mouthpart of an insect such as a common housefly, used for consuming liquid food.

Larva: A young insect that is markedly different from the adult: caterpillars and fly maggots are good examples (plural: larvae).

Mandible: The jaw of an insect. It may be sharply toothed and used for biting, as in grasshoppers and wasps, or it may be drawn out to form a slender needle, as in mosquitoes.

Molt: The shedding of the outer covering of the body, the exoskeleton, during growth.

Nectar: The sugary liquid secreted by many flowers; used by bees to make honey.

Ommatidium: One of the units that makes up the compound eyes of arthropods (plural: ommatidia).

Pheromone: A substance secreted by an animal that sends a message to a receiving individual of the same species; different pheromones can be used for mating and feeding purposes.

Pollen: Microscopic dust from a seed plant, such as a flower, used to reproduce. Many plants rely on bees to distribute pollen.

Predator: An animal that attacks and feeds on other animals that are usually smaller and weaker than itself.

Proboscis: The projecting, sucking organ of a butterfly, similar to the labium of a fly.

Spiracles: The pits or holes on the bodies of certain larvae, such as ladybugs, that are used for breathing.

Vasodilator: A chemical agent that widens blood vessels; usually found in female mosquitoes.

Vibrissae: The pair of large bristles just above the mouth in certain species of flies.